AF583898

TIWI SEASONS WITH MARIUS

To Tiwi College students past, present and future, who become authors.

TIWI COLLEGE

ALALINGUWI JARRAKARLINGA

WITH SHELLEY WARE & DAVID LAWRENCE

Marius is a Tiwi man who loves his culture. He is waiting to welcome his old friend Michael and his son Justin, who are visiting for a year.

They look like they are melting. 'This **tiyari** season is so hot. Good luck to them mob getting off the ferry!' laughs Marius.

It's **tiyari** in October and it's steamy! Marius takes Michael and Justin in the troopy to his camp. '**Parlingarri** we never used to have cars and air con,' Marius says. 'Just open the window, you'll cool down.'

When they arrive, Marius calls out to the old people. This lets them know there are visitors on Country, so they will look after Michael and Justin.

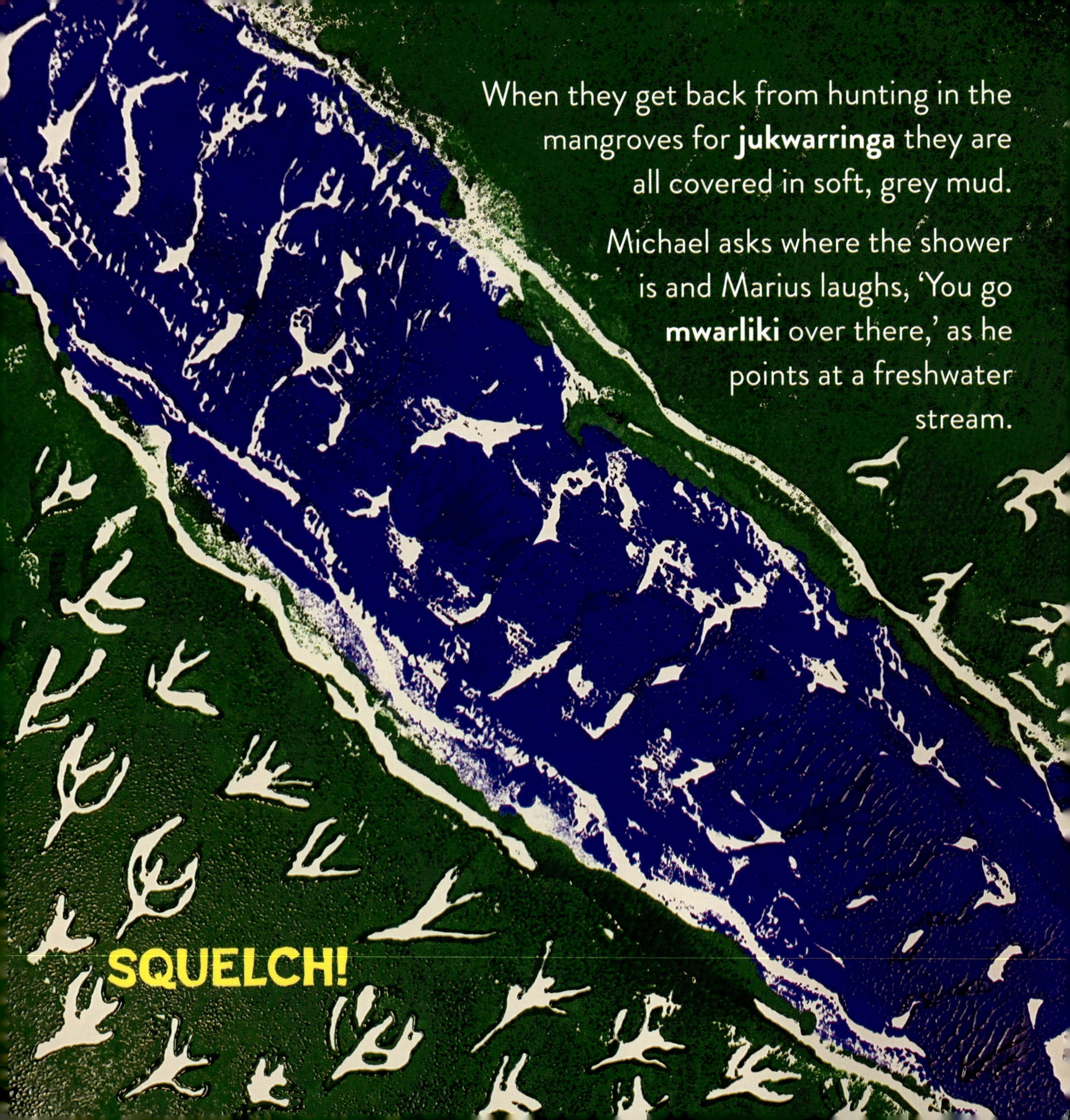

When they get back from hunting in the mangroves for **jukwarringa** they are all covered in soft, grey mud.

Michael asks where the shower is and Marius laughs, 'You go **mwarliki** over there,' as he points at a freshwater stream.

As night settles in, they sit around the campfire. Dingos **HOWL** in the background. Marius teaches them how to dance his totem, jungle fowl. Even though they are terrible dancers, they have the best night.

BOOM!

Black clouds creep towards them. 'It's okay, **jamutakari** season means the rain's coming,' says Marius.

Cold air blows through Justin's blond, curly hair.

The lights all go out.
'Awww man,' says Justin,
'I was watching TikTok.'

Marius calls out to Justin,
'Don't be boring, come
and have fun in the rain.'

Marius kicks a football
to Justin but it slips out of
his hands into the puddle.

SPLAT!

It is January and Marius takes them fishing down the **tingata**. '**OI!** Watch out for crocs and jellyfish!'

Marius catches the biggest barra ever. **'Ngiya pirayayuwu,'** he yells. They wrap it in foil with some lemon and cook it on the fire. The fire **CRACKLES.** The fish smells delicious and tastes even better.

'Ah you know what? Seafood is good in wet season, but you can't eat buffalo and wallaby 'cause they have worms.'

'Eww!' says Justin.

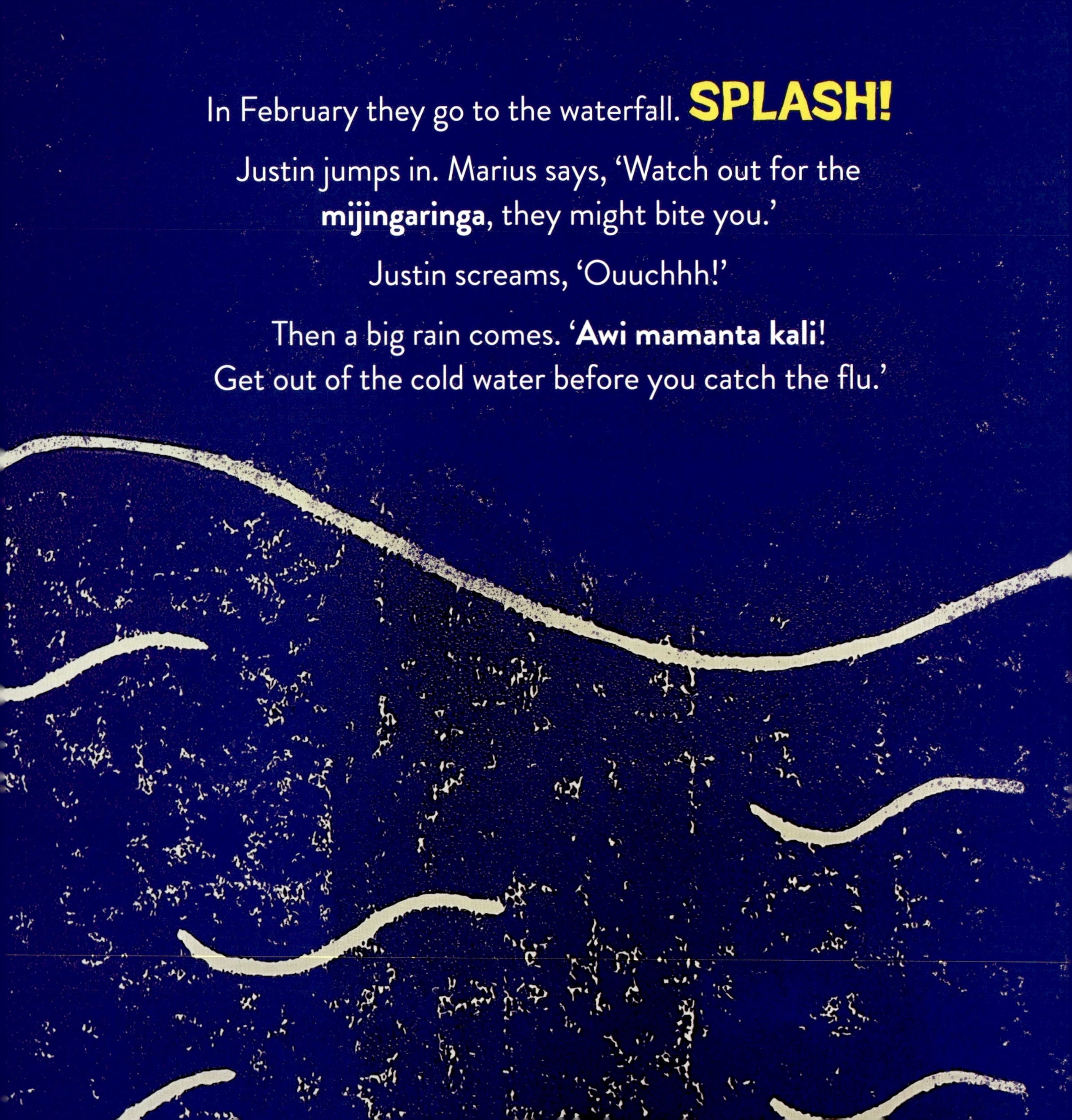

In February they go to the waterfall. **SPLASH!**

Justin jumps in. Marius says, 'Watch out for the **mijingaringa**, they might bite you.'

Justin screams, 'Ouuchhh!'

Then a big rain comes. '**Awi mamanta kali**! Get out of the cold water before you catch the flu.'

WOO!

It's March and the Tiwi grand final is on. Everybody comes in from everywhere. You can hear everyone cheering.

Marius is happy
'cause his team won.
'I support the Tigers
now too,' says Justin.

COUGH, COUGH. It's June and **kumunupunari** season. The weather is cooler and the rangers light fires so the forest can regrow. There is lots of smoke in the sky.

Marius is preparing for a camping trip. 'We're going to catch a carpet snake for dinner.'

He finds a hollow log and places a mirror at one end. '**Kali kali**! I found a big one.' He grabs some dead grass, stuffs it in one end and lights it up. Soon the snake's head slowly pokes out of the log. Quick as a flash, Marius grabs the head of the snake and stuffs it in a bag.

It's August and Justin wants to go swimming in the ocean. '**Arnapa** Justin! Unless you want to get stung by a jellyfish,' says Marius. 'Let's go out on the boat instead.'

'Are you whistling, Marius?' asks Justin.

'No, it's the **marntuwunyini,**' says Marius, pointing to the clear water. Justin sees the trail on top of the water. 'It looks like a giant snake.'

It's the end of the year's stay. So Justin and Michael have a safe journey home, Marius and the Community do a farewell **yoyi**. The men dance and sing the sailing boat song for safe travels, then pass them a **pukumani** pole, for their dreaming **yirrikipayi**, as a parting gift.

What is your favourite Tiwi season?

WORDS IN TIWI

Tiwi seasons

Tiyari – Hot weather season (September to November)

Jamutakari – Wet season (December to February)

Kumunupunari / Kumurrpunarri – Dry season (March to August)

~

Parlingarri – Old days

Jukwarringa – Mud mussels

Mwarliki – Swim

Tingata – Beach

Ngiya pirayayuwu – Good for me!

Mijingaringa – Prawn

Awi mamanta kali – Hey friends, come

Kali kali – Come quickly

Arnapa – Wait

Marntuwunyini – Dugong

Yoyi – Ceremony

Pukumani – Totem pole

Yirrikipayi – Crocodile

There are three main Tiwi seasons as well as 13 minor overlapping seasons.

To see the full seasonal calendar scan the QR code below.

About the Indigenous Literacy Foundation

The Indigenous Literacy Foundation (ILF) is a national charity working with remote Aboriginal and Torres Strait Islander Communities across Australia. We are Community-led, responding to requests from remote Communities for culturally relevant books, including early learning board books, resources, and programs to support Communities to create and publish their stories in languages of their choice.

Text and illustrations produced in 2022 as part of the CREATE program with the Indigenous Literacy Foundation, Hardie Grant Publishing, and Tiwi College Alalinguwi Jarrakarlinga Davina Guy, Crystal Butler, Leontina Puruntatameri, Blanche Lorenzo, Ciara Calma, Lindy Olsen, Winifred Puruntatameri, Caroline Puruntatameri and Hilda Moreen.

First published in 2023 by the Indigenous Literacy Foundation
Level 17, 201 Kent Street
Sydney NSW 2000
ilf.org.au

Cataloguing-in-Publication details are available from the National Library of Australia
www.trove.nla.gov.au

ISBN 9781922592910

Typesetting and design by Hardie Grant Publishing

Printed by 1010 Printing Asia Limited, China